Beyond Your pale

Beyond Your pale
By
Brian Sullivan

# Beyond Your pale

## A
## COLLECTION
## OF
## BIZARRE TRUE STORIES
## STARK REALITY POEMS
## PROFOUND THOUGHTS

By
Brian Sullivan

Published in the United States

1SBN-978-1-7372228-8-0

Copyright 2023

Published by Instant Publishing

# Introduction

PALE: a complete enclosure from which you cannot escape.

This book has no limits.

The profound thoughts will cause you to think in directions you probably have never been before. These will convey unspoken about ideas and feelings.

The true stories could not be even made up by using your wildest imagination.

The poetry is meant to depict the stark reality of the world we live in. It will truly bend your mind.

This book is outside of the normal boundaries of the world we live in, with a no holds barred approach.

Outside the PALE will provide you with a new mind experience.

Get ready for a wild ride.

# Words

When you think about it, words are the most powerful invisible force in our world. They have overturned the empires of old and the super states of the modern era. They influence us, arouse us, pacify us, allow us to use or be used, allow us to visualize what we cannot see, and prevent us from seeing what is real and present in front of us. Our words give our conscious mind tools to use and are the frame of the ideas, visions, and all other thoughts which lurk deep in the subconscious. They have allowed us to communicate in hundreds of different languages throughout time. They are the link to each other for better or worse. The pen is mightier than the sword, and the pen only comes alive through the use of words. Such is the power of words.

## Words

Words and phrases come alive
When men with a desire start to contrive

## Words

Beautiful and sweet sounding they seem
Catering to delusions plus an occasional dream

Hate, fear, love, and compassion
Emotions are played on in a simple fashion
Events of the past are vividly recalled
Experiences recreated–traumatic, large and small

Using his gift of words to describe
The glib tone takes you back to the day your mom died
Your mind now relives that dreadful event
As the preacher uses the experience to cry, "repent"

All the things you did as a little boy
All the heartbreak and all of the joy
Everything that happened to you, both good and bad
Words will take you back to the times you've had

The worries and the anxieties of the present hour
Are brought to the surface of your mind with verbal
    power
Should it be the universal fear of growing old
With a few words, its awful dread can take hold

"Your face has a few lines and wrinkle or two,"
Says the cosmetic salesman, "but this will
Make you fresh as the morning dew"

# Words

Unless you speak good English, have manners and
    social grace
You won't be invited for dinner at the boss's place

Rejection and selection are brought to the fore
Good conversation brings many friends to your door
"Be one of the gang," the leader will extoll
He uses group acceptance to gain control

Words can take us back or illuminate the present
Words can bring us forward to anticipate the pleasant
Words can create an overwhelming effect
Our fate, actions, thoughts and emotions they do direct

# Creative

What exactly does a creative person do when they create? They rearrange. They change the order, size, shape, function and color. They make things different to look at, and they do things differently in general. They trod the lonely road of the unseen and create the dreams of the mind, which we call ideas. They see things other people can't.

Their minds are without limits or a lock. They may be called crazy, a dreamer, a fool, or perhaps even an idol. They do all of these aforementioned things and they also create their life as everyone else does. Everyone's life is a work of art, for better or worse. They create their lives with their thoughts. They become what they think about, again, for better or worse. Creative people may be artists, musicians, inventors, writers, engineers, chemists, and the list goes on, but each create in their own field and in their own ways. The creative ones around us also create a world of unique things. Things to buy, to see, to do, and so forth. The creative people are the ones changing our lives.

# Enjoyable

How many people do you really enjoy being around? Most people that we associate with, we merely tolerate. We only enjoy being around a selective few. We like to be around them because they make us feel good. We feel relaxed. We feel at ease. We can be ourselves. They don't criticize or judge us. They have a sense of humor, which is usually pointed at themselves. They laugh at themselves easily. They don't take themselves too seriously and they know who they are. They are animated, interesting, and enthusiastic.

They seem to enjoy life and others. They are at ease with everyone and try to impress no one. They are modest and humble. They make people laugh. They freely give compliments and emphasize another person's skills and achievement. These are just some of the reasons people like being around enjoyable people. People who are considered enjoyable, take some of their precious time, and they give it to another who may be in need of a little enjoyment.

# Resurrection

Most of us get burned out from time to time. When we do, we are to one degree or another, lifeless. When something happens to us that leaves us drained, empty, and exhausted, we are to a point, living without much life. When we reach a place where we have done our best and nothing happens, we fall into an attitude where we just don't care. Life has a way of draining the vivacity from us at times. We're not dead, but we feel like it.

It is during these times that the qualities of a resurrected person are needed. We need a spark to bring us back to life and overcome our lifelessness behavior whatever it may be from. A resurrected person must always keep a part of themselves in reserve for a time when they become once again burned out, exhausted, drained or emptied, or simply just do not care anymore. Holding onto a mental energy reserve and good attitude will be the only things able to bring us back to life.

# Redemptive

How many times do we get a chance to save somebody? The answer is very few, if any. Saving somebody means that you help them to become redeemed, to change, to turn their life around from misery to happiness. Redeeming somebody usually takes place when they reach out. This comes about in one or two ways. Their retraction and hopelessness cause them to reach out or words from another which touch their heart can cause them to reach out.

When they do reach out for help, they are admitting that they can't do it on their own and they need help. They reach out to you. You can do one of two things; you can reject or accept. When you reject, they may never reach out to anyone again. If you accept them, it's very possible that may save them, save their life. What we don't realize is that people reach out to us all the time, but we don't see it. They ask for our help, but we remain unaware of their need. A redemptive person is aware and responsible.

# Prelude – The Silence

We live in a world of overwhelming noise: cars, construction, etc... and we then add to this din with T.V., radios, stereos, and shouting. Collectively, when all of this is employed, we are unable to think, which may be the point. If we can deaden the thoughts of our mind, then we don't have to cope with any reality, which may come through by pure chance.

Some, if not most, cannot tolerate absolute silence for too long. Our existence seems incomplete unless we have some kind of noise injected into our life. Monks who take the vow of silence and live in a world of quietness must contend to look at their inner self, our world, and the meaning of their existence in the scope of a perspective that brings them into a different dimension.

## The Silence

the blast of deafening music numbs his mind
leading the listener to believe he will find

## Prelude – The Silence

a way to still the thoughts
running through his head
fearing the one thing he has come to dread
SILENCE–the total absence of all noise–
a stillness
revealing a desperate need to fill
emptiness with something greater
making him look at his life
making him listen to the strife
going on in his mind that he so artfully deflects
hiding the fact his life has no purpose and
hoping none will suspect

# The Politician's Delight

This poem may be a tad cynical, but it reveals the two or more faces of the politician. The problem is that we are under the control of these charlatans. Our lives are influenced for better and mostly worse as the result of their actions. The real problem is that society has created them and so is stuck with them. They start at the bottom and prove they will go along to get along. Should they fail this test at anywhere along the way, they are out and out for good. There are so many benefits to an elected office that they will do anything to get it and *anything* to keep it. Their desire is to keep people ignorant and dependent. The fact that they are reelected time after time is proof of their ability to do just that. Do we get what we deserve, or deserve what we get?

## The Politician's Delight

Say what the people want to hear
Say it loud and for God's sake, say it clear

## The Politician's Delight

Speak to the young, promise prosperity for each
Speak to the old, give them nothing but peace

Tell the factory worker he deserves to have more
And tell the capitalist the worker is only a whore
Tell the housewife you're going to cut prices of meat
But tell the farmer it's okay to up the tab on beef

Promise the VFW that we're going to win
Turn around and inform the liberal that war is a sin
Give the white-collar worker a little superiority
To help drown and wipe out his mental inferiority

Say what the people want to hear
Say it loud and for God's sake, say it clear
Promise each of them what they need and desire
Truth is a bummer, the real winner is always a liar

# Persuasive

Persuasive people have but one goal in mind, which is to persuade others to do something which will benefit them in some way. Persuasive people have a way about them. People come under their spell or influence easily, and once under, there is a tendency to believe everything the persuasive one has to say. Persuasive people come in all shapes, sizes, and personality types. They get "turned on by turning people on". They get a vicious thrill from entrancing people much like how the actor receives a thrill from having the audience in the palm of his hand.

Not everyone is taken in by the persuader. There are some who see through him and what he is trying to do. One of the hardest things that a persuasive person has to deal with is rejection by the very people who he is trying to persuade. There is a brutal blow to his ego, which must be then rectified and then supported by acceptance.

Persuasive people who persuade others to do good and positive things are a blessings.

## "Physicist Warns Nuclear Arms Race Can't Be Halted"

There are those who say to us,
An atomic war, there will never be
They say that man has reached a balance
And the very thought of using this weapon is
    inconceivable
We are told of the many horrors in store
And are reassured that this will not come to pass
Nuclear war is impossible, they preach
No one will drop the first bomb, the wise say
We are too humane, too intelligent
Too fearful of the consequences to do that,
but how in the fuck do we explain Hiroshima?

## When They Were Happy

I saw them when they were at their best
I try to forget all of the rest
Memories resurface of when they'd fight
Usually over something so slight
And despite the way they'd go after each other
They were all I had, my father and mother

It was all a blur, how both would shout
And to this day, I'm not sure what about
They called each other unpleasant names,
Since of course both of them were to blame
I loved them both, but the fighting I would hate
And of course, thoughts came much too late
To tell them how much they meant to me
It was something that was not meant to be

They died early, before I could say
Now regret fills my heart each day,
But I recall past weekends, how they searched
For antique bargains like kids at play,
Hours on end, seeking out treasure
How happiness shined beyond measure

## When They Were Happy

There, they entered their own world
No one knew how much they loved each other
But me who shared this time with my father and
    mother

I recall how they would hold each other's hand
and laugh like they were in another land
where there only existed strong love
and now they are in heaven above,
these times were something I would cherish
because they made the bad times simply perish

Their love made an impression in such a way
That I remember it vividly to this very day

# Paramount

If you stand out above all others in any area or endeavor, you will be considered paramount. If as a human being you have put yourself aside, disciplined yourself, and achieved a balance thus knowing who and what you are, then you will be paramount among men. Most people cannot put themselves aside even for brief periods. They lack discipline in most areas and they are often neurotic about something, which throws them off balance and they have no idea of who they are or what they are about. They are not paramount. The main trait in a person who is paramount is that they do not think of themselves that way. They don't act like they are better than others.

They realize they are different, but they don't put people down just so they can be above. They have a true humility about themselves. They are able to see other people's side and points of view since they are able to put their own needs, wants, and desires aside. People realize when they are in the presence of a paramount person, and they don't even have to say a word.

# Trust

Can we trust ourselves? Yes, we can trust ourselves to do what makes us feel good. Can we trust other people? Yes, we can trust other people to do what makes them feel good. We can only hope we are both in unison. We must trust in order to have any harmony in our lives. The trick is to rightly know the degree we can trust. It could be 5%, 25%, or 75% and any other number between 99%. We can never trust 100% because who we have to trust is a human being, capable of anything and of anything happening to that person.

There are those who are known as trustworthy. The problem is people are subject to change and because they think 2,000-3,000 thoughts per hour. Any one of those thoughts could change the way they behave and think. If we are to trust ourselves, we must know ourselves for who and what we are. The good, the bad, and the ugly. It's only then that we may take a chance and trust ourselves. We must know the good, the bad, and the ugly in others. It's all there. Don't kid yourself about anyone. They can be capable of doing

# Trust

anything and so can you. Don't trust anything you see and only 50% of actions. You can trust God, and you can trust no matter how hard it is to trust, that things happen for the best.

What is more important than trust?
It's beyond important, it's a must
Therefore, upon it we must always insist
Since life without it becomes a dewy mist
We are unable to see clear
Who we love and those we hold dear

We can't see trust or hold it, but without it we cannot
   hear
That little voice inside telling us danger is near
So we must rely on trust which should be all-seeing
But we can't do that because they are a heinous being,
Which means they are imperfect and always desire
Something we don't know, thus leaving us in a
   quagmire
Of what to do when we need it the most
We still can't hold or see it, and trust becomes a ghost

No matter how hard we try not to doubt
Something inside of us will rise up and shout
Please God, tell me who and what I can trust
God answers only those without judgment, ego, greed
   or lust

# Trustworthy

How do we know if someone is worthy of our trust? Sometimes it's easy to tell right away, and then it can take a period of time for someone to gain our trust. It really depends on the person. Some people are naturally trustworthy and then some have to prove themselves to be worthy of our trust. Once a person is considered to be trustworthy, then it is necessary to in fact trust them with all things.

Then there are some people who can be trustworthy with one thing, such as money, but cannot be trustworthy when it comes to being on time, for example. We still have to pick and choose who we trust to do what. Trustworthy people would do anything not to lose the trust placed in them. They pride themselves on being trusted. It becomes an important part of their personal integrity, and they usually don't betray a trust. They are dedicated to those who trust me, and they take great pride in it. While trustworthy people are hard to find, a friend who proves to be trustworthy is a friend you will have for life.

# Morgue Humor

The Allegheny County Morgue was a huge Graystone building dating back to the 1800s. It had a two-door entrance which led into the chapel. This is where the bodies could be seen and identified. It had a high vaulted ceiling with a stained-glass mural on the back wall and going up to the ceiling. On each side of the chapel were slanted glass enclosures, which opened from the back. The bodies were rolled into the glass enclosure where they could be viewed. People could stand at the foot of the enclosure and see the bodies. Anyone could come in almost any time. Sometimes after a party, a gang from the party who had too much alcohol already would go down to the morgue. There were also chaperoned visits by various scout troops. A reporter from the local paper had the morgue as one of his "beats". He would go down to the morgue and sit around and talk with the guys who worked there. They had a fantastic sense of humor. I guess they had to. This particular reporter liked to play pranks. He would get on a gurney and have the morgue guy roll him under the glass. When someone or a group would come in, he would wink at them or turn his head. People would run out of the place screaming.

He was sitting around with the guys one day when they were told that a girl scout troop was coming down to see the morgue. Here was his chance. He could scare the hell out of a bunch of young girls, so he got on a gurney and had them wheel him under the glass. He had been under for a couple of minutes when a new guy came in. It was his first day. The reporter had never seen him. The morgue guys started talking and someone suggested that the reporter deserved a little karma, so the new guy got on a gurney and they wheeled him in right next to the reporter.

The reporter and the new guy were laying there for a little while when the new guy turned his head to the side and said to the reporter, "Cold as hell in here, ain't it?"

The reporter was so shocked that he sat up too hard and fast and he hit his head on the glass and actually suffered a concussion. He was so dazed he fell off of the gurney and was scrambling around on the floor. The new guy said, "I bet that hurt." This threw the reporter into a panic so he began screaming and pounding on the door, which could only be opened from the outside. The doors didn't open for a few minutes since the morgue guys were laughing so hard they were rolling on the floor. When he did finally get out, he was babbling incoherently and couldn't stop shaking and twitching. It took more than a few stiff drinks to calm him down. Needless to say, he never went under the glass again.

# Spirited

What can we say about those who are "spirited"? Could it be said that somehow the essence of our being, which is our spirit, predominates and takes us over?

If and when this does occur, how much does our spirit enter into our life? Do we become stranger, better, greater or smarter as a result of our spirit "coming out"? We know that spirited people are animated, vigorous and courageous. It appears that something takes time to develop on a spiritual level. Spirted people are almost always positive and upbeat. They tend to look on the bright side.

They are also very persistent and will not take no for an answer. The also influence others through their example, yet they are humble in most instances. If spirited people do let their spirt take over their lives, they will enjoy their life more and make sure to live every second of every minute. Spirited people love life, and they love what they do, whatever it is. Spirted people live their lives to the fullest.

# Daring

The world belongs to the daring. Only those who have the courage to take risks and venture out into the unknown can have power. The weak and the timid are under the control of the daring. They do truly dare to be great or wealthy or successful. They are bold in their thinking and it translates into their action and patterns of behavior. They are willing to go where others fear to tread. They are bold enough to imagine and then turn their imagination into reality.

Only those who can see the invisible can do the impossible. The daring have a bold mindset that has to inhibitions. Daring people think differently; they think bigger and without limits. They see no limits when they look into their dreams. They take those dreams and do what's needed to make them into reality.

Daring people come from all walks of life, from the professional and intellectual to the blue collar and housewives. They all have the same thing in common: They have a desire to look better and do better. They dare to follow those wishes and ideas to completion.

# All of My Life

"All my life my heart has
sought a thing I cannot name"

During the 60s when the Vietnam war was raging, there
was another being waged on the home front. The children
of the men who had come from WWII, were now coming
of age. They had grown up in a world of plenty; they were
given material things like no other generation before them.
They indulged themselves in physical pleasures to no end.
Yet it was not enough to satisfy something lurking inside
of them. They sought a cause and found one. They sought
different ways of life and found them only to keep coming
up empty. They tried every drug there was only to find temporary relief, but it wasn't what they were looking for. They
formed families. They needed a family no matter how un-
reliable other members of the family were. These families
all lived in a certain part of town in rundown apartments
and old homes.

## All of My Life

The author of this poem lived in one of those rundown buildings, inhabited by more than a few families. In one of these apartments where the author lived, there was a piece of blue art paper written in white with sequins on the lettering, which read "All my life my heart has sought a thing I cannot name."

This seemed to sum up what this generation was looking for. They didn't know and never found out. They eventually drifted back into normal lives with wives, kids, and a lot of responsibilities. This poem illustrates their predicament at that time in their lives.

# All of My Life

All of my life my heart has sought a thing I cannot
    name
My heart is always restless and refuses to be tame
My heart is always looking to know
My mind constantly wonders to and fro
I know that I am not the only soul
Millions of others are desperately seeking the goal

Of what their heart wishes them to be
Working in vain for the one thing they cannot see

We all move around in a daze
Minds clouded by a never-ending hope
We sometimes think we know which ways
To go in order to find where answers lie
A place deep in our subconscious mind
Where even we dare not to go

Yet we try to plunge those darkest depths
And search in utter futility only to find
That the real answer will always elude us
But we continue on and on because we must
We constantly prod ourselves
And never give up this futile game
Only to find out that all of my life
My heart has sought a thing I cannot name

# Unselfish

What a thrill to encounter a truly unselfish person. One who thinks of others before they think of themselves. An unselfish person is one who has conquered his own basic human nature and got past themselves. Our basic human nature is selfish. Our physical makeup has been designed to be selfish. We have to provide the body with energy through food, keep certain temperatures so the body can survive, and also keep the mind entertained. All of these elements cause us to focus on our basic needs out of pure necessity. This then becomes a habit to focus on one's self, and to care for the basic needs, and then beyond the basic needs to what can be called the luxuries of life: Money, cars, entertainment, material things, fame, prestige, ego, satisfaction and other pleasures.

In combination, these things make people almost guaranteed to be totally selfish. It's their basic nature; so, when someone breaks the pattern and moves past their own needs and wants, and they are able to see others as just as important, it is contrary to our natural instincts and it is anything but common.

# Collected

How does one achieve the status of being "calm, cool, and collected"? How does one collect these thoughts? Does calm and cool go along with being collected? Are they one and the same?

Collected usually means that a person's integrity is intact and they are functioning well. If is a person is collected, they will be calm and cool. They will be impervious to situations that would excite a lot of people. A collected person is also a very objective person normally, but there are of course exceptions. A collected person has control over their emotions, which is one of the reasons they are collected. Collecting one's thoughts and values means calming the mind and putting thoughts into a logical sequence where they are coherent and make sense. A collected person can be counted on to prevail in a difficult situation that calls for a cool head and self-control. Collected equals self-control.

# Life Begins at 40

We all change. Some changes are for the better, some for the worst. As we grow older, hopefully we change for the better. Our younger years are the learning years, and when you learn, usually by your mistakes, you are forced to either change or continue to make the same mistakes. Hopefully by the age of 40 you have learned and changed enough that now, with a lot of the hard learning over, you can begin to enjoy life instead of going through the trial and error, which everyone goes through.

Life could also begin at 50, 60, 30 or whatever age you are at when you finally realize that what you know now along with a desire to really live and completely change, can be the beginning of your best years. Plus, the truth is that age is a state of mind. We could begin our life whenever we choose to begin it, no matter what age we are at. Our life begins when we find the joy of living in everything we do.

# Homer's Love Life

This is another true story where the names have been changed for the sake of the living relatives.

Let me tell you about Homer. He was a short, fat, bald-headed guy, and he was not what you would call good looking. He worked all of his life in one job – a mechanic on the railroad. He fell in love with a girl of beauty named Angela. They planned to get married. A deep true love on both parts. Her father felt that Homer was not worthy of his daughter so he sent her abroad to study. After having lost the love of his life, Homer wound up getting married to an older woman. She died. Homer then married another older woman. She died. Homer then gave it another shot and he married another older woman. Number three also died. He turned 65 after number three passed from this world. He was retired and lonely. During all this time, Homer and Angela were exchanging passionate love letters.

Now in his sixties, he met Ruth who owned an antique shop and got married again. Number four. Ruth was a little frumpy, but that didn't stop her from becoming a successful business woman. She opened up two more stores in different parts of the state. This took her away from home and Homer most of the time. Homer was lonely again. He and Angela were still writing passionate love letters to one another expressing desires which neither would ever be able to achieve. Angela had married a Texas oil man who had gone to that great oil field in the sky. He left her well-off. She wrote Homer and told him it was time for them to be together. She told him she would buy him a new Cadillac and they would live together in her upscale home with no money worries. She sent him the money and he bought himself a new DeVille. He deeded the house to Ruth, gave her all the money, got into his new Caddy and drove to Texas.

It's an old saying but it's true, there is no fury like a woman scorned. Ruth got into her car and drove to Texas. When she got there, much to the chagrin of Homer and Angela, she set up camp in their front yard and refused to move. This could not go on forever, and finally went to court.

Ruth sued for alienation of affection. This was the state's record for people of that age to sue for the alienation of affection. There they were. Two women in their seventies fighting over a fat, aged, balding man who was never considered to have good looks. This was the comedy of comedies. There was not a dry eye in the court including the judge and jury.

Ruth won and Angela was glad to agree to a generous settlement. Homer divorced Ruth and married Angela, the love of his life. Marriage number five. Angela and Homer lived together for several blissful years. Angela made their funeral preparations. She bought two graves side by side and a dual headstone with her name on one side and Homer on the other side. Angela died. Ruth found a home in Texas and lived there. Homer was by himself and was lonely once more. Homer could not stand to be alone. He was cursed with a need to have someone in his life, no matter who.

He started seeing Ruth and eventually they got married, again. This was number six for Homer. This would be his last. Homer died. Ruth has also made preparation for their final remains, two lots and a dual headstone for her and Homer. Ruth had Homer's body flown back up north and buried in the plot she had prepared for. When she died, Homer would be next to her. Remember, hell hath no fury like a woman scorned. He was her man in life and death. Homer and Angela were destined to be apart in death as they had been in life. They were the loves of each other lives, but this for whatever reason, was to be their destiny.

# Never Put Off Until Tomorrow What You Can Do Today

Mortality tells us there may be no tomorrow, although almost all of us end up dismissing this and take the idea of tomorrow for granted, as in "I'll see you tomorrow". For some people, that tomorrow will never come, and that will happen to all of us eventually. What we assume would take place tomorrow, can never take place one day.

What is even more tragic is when two people who are in love part hurriedly with the intention of expressing their love and showing their affection to each other later, and one of them never sees tomorrow. True love doesn't tolerate procrastination. Don't wait until another time if you love someone, now and only now is the time to tell them. Procrastination in all things leads to frustration. Procrastination will end up just providing chaos in one's life. Procrastination is fear and insecurity, which contributes to a sense of low self-esteem. There is no magic formula for overcoming procrastination, but we can try to develop a set of incentives to overcome the hesitation.

# Keeping the Meaning in Life

What is the meaning of life? We've all asked that question at one time or another. Perhaps the question should be what is life without meaning? The answer is simple, nothing. This question in turns begs another question: How do we keep meaning in our life if life is nothing without meaning?

The things of meaning in our life can be put into four categories: Ourselves, others, things, and God. Should the meaning of our life be things or ourselves, it will only be a matter of time before we hit rock bottom of the two due to superficial and selfish ends. Should the meaning of our life lie with other people, there will come a time when people let us down no matter how reliable or unselfish our purpose is in making others our life.

This leaves only one, God. We can see, feel and touch the other three; we can't see or touch God. We must go back to the days of our childhood and have a simple faith in God, a no questions asked kind of belief. God must become as real to us as the other three.

The other three have limits. We can only love ourselves so much, can only have so many things, and others can only love us so much. None of them will make do. The meaning of our life must be tied to something that has no bottom, no limits. When we believe in something that is limitless, then and only then will we continue to have meaning in our lives no matter what the world brings down upon us.

# Prelude – Left and Right

They are different. They are the same. Endless hours are spent arguing which is right. No decision has been reached. No decision ever will be reached. The deciding factor will always be who achieved power. People are used like pawns in their quest to gain and retain power. Either one will use almost any means to accomplish this. We can be sure of only one thing, and that is our life is for us to determine, no one else.

This poem points out that as much as they are different, they all have one aim, power, raw power and nothing else.

## Left and Right

Left and right, there's a difference
Some people will say, one is good,
Or the other is bad
Liberalism and conservatism
Are as to day is to night, more or less

### Prelude – Left and Right

There is a difference, that part is true
That difference is the same as me and you
Use your talents, pick your brain
Their programs are varied, the ends the same
Control your body and mind, thoughts and deeds
The difference of the three is who runs the game

Organize, consolidate, manipulate and stimulate
Play one side against the other, ignorance is the wedge
See all, know all, do all, and control all
Indoctrinate, condition, decondition and recondition

Inhibit and mistreat our movements of body and soul
Automate and accelerate our will to live on and on
Delude and exclude all those who deviate from the chosen
    path
Bend or break and regiment all wills for total control

Create a crisis, encourage conflict, jeopardize
A way of life, threaten existence to its core
Then solve the problem, erase the doubt
Ease anxiety, but first take all you want, plus a little
    more

Smash and bash the bones of those very few
Who dare to be different from the ever common millions
Power is power and who has it is of little concern
They will do anything to keep it, that you will soon
    learn

# Unmistakable

Some people have such a distinct personality that they are unmistakable. You cannot possibly mistake them for someone else. There are different in so many ways that it is impossible to confuse them with anybody else. Unmistakable people are generally known to take pride in the fact that they are so different as to distinguish them from all others. They have become their own creation and usually don't care how others regard them.

This can be a very positive or a very negative thing. If they are obnoxious, hostile, arrogant or mean spirited, then people will avoid them like the plague; however, on the positive side, they can be charming, different yet interactive and delightfully unique in their personality and generally outlook. Unmistakable people have no need to resort to attention getting behavior. Their personality usually gives them all the attention they need.

Unmistakable people add color to what can be at times a drab world.

# Racing to Red Lights

We see them every day racing as fast as they can, even when they see the light is red, then slamming on the brakes to avoid hitting the car in front of them who is still waiting for the light to change. When the light turns green, the next race is on. What we may ask is the cause of such madness. Could it be they are in such a hurry that good sense has abandoned them, or could it be that they live at such a frantic pace that they do everything in their life with the same intensity. We don't know, but what we do know is that they are blind to everyone and everything around them. Hopefully this poem captures reckless abandon and the absolute feeling of those who endanger the lives of others as well as themselves.

## Racing to Red Lights

Drivers grasp the wheel with great intensity
Impulses racing on, relentless

## Racing to Red Lights

They look neither to the left or right
Because of other people, they have lost sight
Consumed with only one desire
To reach their destination, they burn with a fire

They speed ahead faster and faster
Ignoring fate and courting disaster
They pass other cars, weave out and in
They literally fly down the street like the wind

They have beaten every car, let none stand in their way
They raced to the red light and won the day
Gunning their engines, they are now ready
For the next race their look is intense and steady

So focused on being first
Yet ignorance wins,
And the feeling of their quest
Is nothing more than a curse

# Sparkling

Some people light up a room just by being themself. You know when they enter the room that something about them is different. They have a sparkling personality that is radiant. They radiate confidence, joy, and good humor. They seem to bowl people over with the power of their effervescent personality. People automatically gravitate toward them. They attract almost everyone.

They are a pleasure to be around because they make people not only feel good, but also alive. They are beyond being positive. They cannot even conjure a negative thought much less an attitude. Their enthusiasm seems to be contagious. People leave them feeling better. Sparkling people usually are the center of any party or get-together. They are outgoing and extroverted, full of a sense of adventure. They make friends easily since most people like to be friendly with them. They are always outwardly happy or seek to be even when they may be feeling low inside.

Sparkling people are more than the life of the party, they are the magic of the party.

# Valentine's Day

At least there is one day in the year devoted entirely to love. This day presents the perfect opportunity to say, "I love you" in a number of ways – a card, dinner, a special treat or something as simple as breakfast in bed. On this day, the initial onus is on the man. He's the one who gets the flowers, buys the candy, sends the card and takes someone to dinner. The woman reciprocates by verbalisms, and expressing her love and thanks. She might add how lucky she is to love such a wonderful mate. This is optional of course.

For those men foolish enough to ignore this one day love ritual, resentment by the ton is carted off to the storehouse of the woman's mind, easily retrieved at a moment's notice and used as a lethal verbal weapon in the swift denial of any sort of favors. Tone, being mostly a perception, is subject to what is perceived. Tone is also a state of mind, which again is subject to perception. For many, love is only an illusion,

## Valentine's Day

something they believe they feel when in actuality it has no substance. True love is deep and unselfish.

Valentine's Day caters to loves of all kind, real and illusion and perception deep and shallow.

# Specific

Plainspoken would be an accurate way of describing specific people. They are exact in what they are saying and leave no doubt as to the true meaning. They hone in on a point and isolate it so others know exactly what they mean. They are not capable of speaking of generalities. They are never vague. Their meanings are never clouded, and are always clear.

They are not only clear, they are very definitive in what they say. They are specific so they can make a point that cannot be refuted. Their specific reasons are made to reduce a complex subject to simple terms by breaking it down to something easily understandable. Specific points are made to clarify things which could be construed in a number of ways.

Specific people have a compulsion to make people understand what they say. This is not to say that all people who are specific fall in this category. Some people can be specific about something without the neurotic tendency that demands they be understood.

# A Forlorn Life

Negative people are to be found everywhere. Some are religious people who faithfully go to church. Nothing their clergy says touches them. They remain negative and vindictive, unable to truly love or care about anyone, even themselves. Thus, they go through life leading a joyless and barren existence. They probably have never even given a thought to the meaning of their life. All lives have a meaning even if they seem not to have one. At the end of her life all she had believed in was exposed to be untrue. What she thought was enough wasn't. When she thought she was living a "good" life, she wasn't. When it finally dawned on her that life was also about other people, it was too late. The tragedy was not realizing and knowing this until it was too late. She died a very forlorn woman.

# The Good Woman

The good woman represents part of society. They live their daily lives doing a little good, and maybe doing only small bad things. Bad things such as gossip an unkind word, judgmental of other people, envy, and some greed as well. Their lives are for the most part meaningless. They consider themselves good people since they have never done anything so wrong that they got arrested or did prison time. They die wondering what it was all about. They say they believe in God, but never go to church or even think of the simple adage of "Do unto others as you would have them do unto you." Everyone makes a choice of how to live their life. The "Good" woman has inadvertently chosen a life which goes nowhere.

> The corners of her mouth turned down
> Her face wore nothing but a total frown
> She saw the negative parts of life,
> Continually found something about which to gripe

## The Good Woman

Quick to condemn and impossible to please
Always wondering why she was all at ease
Suspicion and mistrust were all she knew
The years went by and her hostility grew

"They ought to be put away"
"God will surely punish them someday"
She uttered these words against many people
A good Christian woman who sat under God's steeple

She felt that because she broke no laws
That she was a good person with minor flaws
She sat in her house and talked about
Anyone whose reputation was in doubt

The day finally came to pass
When the life was leaving her fast,
"I've been a good woman all my time
I've never done wrong or committed a crime"

"Exactly what have you done?" asked a voice
"Did you help or turn away when you had a choice?
You've done nothing with your life but be
Heaven and happiness are for those who do good, you
    see"

# Preservation

Everyone has something good and valuable inside of them, even those who we consider the worst of people have something worthwhile about them. Preservation is keeping safe that which is good about yourself. If you are a generous person, then it would be in your best interest to preserve that trait of generosity and not let greed enter into your thoughts, life, or actions. Nothing should stop you from keeping a very positive trait as opposed to becoming greedy, which is a very negative state to be in.

Another example is a person who is peaceful. Sometimes, given the situation, it could be all too easy to react in a violent way. The peaceful part of that nature should be retrieved and kept intact, for once someone starts down the path of violence, it is too easy to solve all problems simply by eliminating them. Preservations are designed to keep the best parts of us intact and free from the inclination to resort to behavior which would harm and eventually eliminate the best parts of ourselves.

## Preservation

Situations become something that have the power to change us and could cause us to do things, which under normal circumstances, we would not even consider doing. Preservation of our good traits cannot be accomplished unless we are aware of the power of situations to change us.

When we make a conscious choice to reserve the best part of us, no matter what, we will preserve.

# Forgiveness

Forgiveness is contrary to our human nature, which demands that we get even or get the best of any kind of pain that has been inflicted upon us by another. In fact, what is known as the "get even mechanism" is probably man's second strongest instinct and forms a primary part of his human nature. The "get even mechanism" is so strong that it overrides logic, reason, common sense, morality, and even our own best interests.

Forgiveness is the exact opposite of "get even" and is therefore contrary to an important part of our basic human nature. Forgiveness is not only giving up the desire to get even, it goes further and excuses any wrong through renouncing anger and resentment. Since it is not natural to do this, it must be done with an act of the will in conjunction with a change of heart that allows you to erase it from your consciousness as though it never happened.

Getting even or harboring hate and resentment will result in bitterness and prevent a true happiness. Letting go

## Forgiveness

of all thoughts of getting even and all thoughts of hate or resentment will not only free you, it will allow your heart to be filled with a special kind of joy.

# Light

"I've never seen the light" is a common expression indicating that someone now has a deep understanding of something that had previously eluded them. "Don't keep me in the dark" is often heard when someone feels that something is being kept from them, which they need to know. Dark covers and hides things. Light allows things to be seen clearly for what they really are.

Seeing the light is usually referred to in connection to a spiritual awakening where a person comes to the realization that the best part of him is his essence within himself, his spirit. When he knows what is real about him cannot be seen on the outside, but rather felt by a deep feeling inside, then it can be said that he has seen the light. He has caught a glimpse of the light of his soul. He is now considered enlightened.

Someone who has seen the light and understands the reality of their being has experienced a drastic change in their

## Light

life. What they considered important before is now of little or no value to them. What they had overlooked, their own spirituality, is now the center and core of their being. They are now in the light.

# A Kleptomaniac is Born

Another true story. It's a shaggy dog story, but it's true. Phil was a generous man. You might even say he was overly generous. He had a beautiful wife and wonderful family, fame, a great career, and of course money. He also had a partner is his business. Dan and Phil were a great pair and created a very unique business. They were so successful that Phil was featured on the cover of national magazines.

This all came cracking down one fateful night. Phil and Dan got into a real brawl in a hotel. This was complete with screaming, broken furniture, and lamps through a window. Things calmed down and Dan called Phil's wife. Phil was a very personable guy and also a prolific womanizer. Unbeknownst to Phil, Dan had kept record of each affair complete with name, date, and location of each tryst. When he got Phil's wife on the phone, he proceeded to read off the entire list. He then handed the phone to Phil. His wife asked him if this was true. Phil was not known for being the most truthful of people, but this time he told the truth, and confessed all. The partnership was dissolved. Phil in one fell swoop lost his business, his family, and his mind. He had to be confined to a mental institution.

He came out a different person. He was angry. He would rage and he would steal and "walk" checks in restaurants. It didn't matter what it was or even if he needed it. He would steal anything from "please be seated" signs to waste baskets, pens, books, and virtually anything he saw. He was still a womanizer, but he would insult and humiliate the women he was with. He would nickname them with the names and introduce them that way as the horse, the fox, the gopher, and so on. He upset a woman so bad one time that her eyes rolled to the back of her head and all you saw were the whites of her eyes. When the waiter came with the tray of food and saw only the whites of her eyes, he dropped the whole tray on the table.

It seemed Phil felt that since everything had been stolen from him, his business, his wife, and family as well as his reputation and fame, that it was only right to steal back what he could and he became a diehard kleptomaniac.

He stole everything he could by his hand and he did however get his comeuppance when it came to women. He met a widow who was a first-grade teacher before she retired. She saw something in him and they got married. True to form, he would rage and insult her. She would ignore him and say things like, "Now you don't mean that, Phil." He could not upset her. When asked the question of how she was able to

## A Kleptomaniac is Born

deal with him when no one else could, she would answer that she would just treat him like she did her first graders. The rage ended but every once in a while, the kleptomania would surface. He never felt that he had gotten even.

# Glorious

Glorious people seem to shine. They emit something that is so striking to others that they stand in a state of awe, as though entranced. Their eyes seem to attract people automatically to them. There is something about them that is magnetic. They appear to be magnificent in every way they walk, talk, and look. People whom one would conclude glorious stand out in any crowd. The question is what makes them glorious?

The one thing for sure is that what it is, it is significant and contained within them. It permeates their being and flows outward. It touches people by its beauty of the soul. It is delightful to just be around this person, for they have the ability to make people warm and feel good about themselves. This is probably the most glorious thing of all that when people are touched by their presence, they feel like better people, too. Even if that feeling is only for a short period of time before they revert back to their typical behavior, it is a significant moment.

Glorious people light up the world and other people in special, memorable ways.

# Socrates

Socrates was convinced of the immortality of the soul. He believed that this was the core of man's being and that nothing else made any sense in the grand scheme of things. He projected that for man to achieve harmony, he must first be virtuous. He must be just, honest, and have the courage to do what is right. He believed that unless man believed in the immortality of his own soul, there was little or no reason to lead a life of virtue, which in turn leads to harmony with his fellow man.

A man who does not believe in the immortality of the soul will turn to a life of vice since there is nothing after death, then one must enjoy life to the fullest even at the expense of others. This produces a world of disharmony, conflict, and confusion. Socrates looked forward to his death for he believed that the soul would come into the presence of the great good and would live forever in a state of harmony and bliss.

# Despair and Depression

There isn't a person in this entire world who at one time or another hasn't been in the depths of despair and depression because of circumstances and events which seem to be beyond their capacity to deal with. Most turn their efforts into constructive chances and climb out of the mental morass. Some don't and more lives are wasted, and negative thoughts continue to dominate. Thousands of words have been written in verse and prose to inspire man to overcome his mental dilemma and love life and be happy again. These few lines are written for the person who is so down that the bottom looks like up, and if only one person on this planet reads this and breaks his chains of depression slavery, it will have served its purpose.

Fear clings to his every pore
Despair is with him evermore

## Despair and Depression

Anxiety forms a cloud above his head
Failure is a constant and awesome dread

He is down and he is out
Of this there can be no doubt
The bottom has finally been reached
His contract with life pitifully breached

He looks around for friend or hope
Problems haunt him, unable to cope
No family, no friends, no way to go
Just a broken man who has hit his low

Negatives have torn him down
Reduced his face to a perpetual frown
Until one day he noticed a man in similar plight
The only difference was the other had lost his sight

Into his world of negatives was he thrust
A positive thought that things could be worse
A smile found its way upon his face
A positive deed was about to take place

# Selfishness

Selfishness is the mother of all evil and the creator of all sins, for when a person is selfish, no thought is given to other people. This allows the selfish person to do as they please without regard to the effect on others. Thus, they can indulge themselves in any behavior which benefits them regardless of the cost to others. This can be done on a large scale such as the military industrial complex starting a war in order to increase production and make money at the expense of the population as a whole. Or it could be someone who takes a handicapped parking space because they don't want to take a few extra steps to the store.

They totally disregard the handicapped people who do need a spot and take care of their own selfish wants instead. The more they descend into selfish patterns of behavior, the less they care about others. They will become immersed in material things and buy everything they can, not because they need it, but to satisfy selfish needs, wants and desires. Selfish people are easy to spot and when you do, stay as far away from them as you can.

# The Wooden Pillow

Death and life all run together. They both serve an end and a purpose of which we may only be vaguely aware of, no matter what we may think and believe. Our end and purpose into a grand plan and design which we cannot even begin to understand. We are given life and promised death. We are promised nothing else in between. What happens between is a matter of choice, fate, and destiny, all of which comprise the in-between. The in-between is what gives our life meaning or little to no meaning, but all lives have a meaning of some kind. The "Wooden Pillow" follows the course of everyone's life to one degree or another. The thing no man can avoid and the thing all men crave and then the finale, the grave.

## Wooden Pillow

A wooden pillow sat placed beneath his head
A wooden pillow was used because he was dead

## The Wooden Pillow

The life and spark all gone out
One more being who can't move about

His life was short, a little bitter, a little sweet
But all that's over now since he's under a sheet
He never realized what life really meant
The years flew by and suddenly his time was spent

His face remains bland in death, as in life
Human nature destined him to constant strife
His soul and mind became numb after awhile
Then it was he who could do to fake a smile

He bounced back and forth from pleasure to pain
Like a ping pong ball during a rather fast game
His greed and lust pursued momentary pleasure
His fear and ignorance caused pain he couldn't measure

Most of his life was lived in vain
Most of his time spent avoiding pain
He took and took, and only gave
Something that wasn't wanted or he couldn't save

# Realness

What has happened in a person's life that makes him a real person as opposed to a fake person? What experiences have directed him toward being a genuine person with character as opposed to someone who is not real? Was he born that way or did he somehow develop to that end? How did his parents determine that or other people in his life?

The real person began to make decisions early in life that led him to becoming he is today. He lacked fear because fear will cause you to hide behind a mask to protect you from the reality of the revelation.

He had self-esteem. He liked who he was. He had pride in who he was. A lack of self-esteem will cause others to pretend to be something they're not so they gain recognition and even more importantly, acceptance. If you don't have pride in who and what you are then you will create a fictional character that you can be proud of. However, this character and the pretense that goes along with it are not real.

Real people have no need to pretend.

# Prelude – I'll Never Forget You God

Many of us are destined to lose our memories through the disease of Alzheimer's. There may be nothing we can do to prevent that, but if we make a vow never to forget God and surround ourselves with the signs of him, a cross, a bible, a picture of God that Da Vinci painted in the Sistine Chapel, a picture of Jesus at the Last Supper, and put into our minds what each of these represents, then perhaps His will be the only memory we have left. It's important that God is with us in mind and spirit to the very end.

## I'll Never Forget You God

As our life comes toward its end
Our minds begin to lose something
Then start to blend past with present
Forgetting much of what was

## Prelude – I'll Never Forget You God

The thoughts we allow to stay with us
No matter what comes into our life,
We make a vow to never forget the ones
We love and cherish as we grow old
But most of all, we'll never be told
That we forgot God because we'll promise,
"I'll never forget you God"

No matter how much my memory dims
How could I ever forget you after all you have done
You gave me life and let me live under your sun
You were there when I needed you
You were there when I was happy and when I was blue
You knew my heart and were forgiving
Of all my sins and all my sinful living, too
How could I ever forget you?
When only you were the one who knew
The things that held my deepest regrets
And you were the one who forgave me of my debts
I'll never forget you God, this I vow
I make this promise to you here and now

One time, he reached down to help a man lower than he
"Let me help you," he said to the one who couldn't see
He lifted his brother up to his feet
And realized then that he was far from beat

Now he knew he could always find
An optimistic thought to think

## Prelude – I'll Never Forget You God

He was also aware that a positive deed was the link
In the chain of life of which he was a part
A positive thought and deed is where you can start

# Sincere

Sincere people have a real problem telling a lie. They seem incapable of being able to be anything but sincere. They are not only true to themselves, they can't help but be true to others. Unless you want to hear what they truly believe, do not ask a sincere person anything. They will be honest with you.

Sincere people also make the best teachers as they have an innate desire to help people. They are natural and unaffected and free from the hypocrisy that seems to dominate our world. They convey a depth of feeling rather than superficial or feigned emotions.

They are genuine to the core and not afraid to express this true feeling or to reveal their true nature. They have a depth to them that is apparent to anyone who takes the time to get to know them. They can always be counted on to put forth their best effort as well as being honest in their dealing. A sincere friend will never ever let you down.

# Spirit

The essence of our being is spirit. We all have it. Some will say, "He has a strong spirit." It follows that if this is true, then others might have a weak spirit. The spirit is connected to the life within us, so if our physical and mental make-up is strong, it would likely make our spirit strong – so it would seem. However, what if the strength of our spirit comes from another source? Is it possible that the strength of our spirit comes from an even greater spirit that imbues our spirit with extraordinary strength?

Should this be true, how do we get connected with this all powerful spirit? We must first believe that such a spirit does exist, and that it contains a power over us that is also somehow a part of us. Once we believe, then we must let go and allow the powerful spirit flow into us. We may not be able to feel this happen. There may be no outward signs of this taking place. This is where the power of faith comes into play. When we believe in something greater than we are and have faith in this greater spirit, we become part of it.

# Only So Many Years

We can't see time, but we can spend it or waste it, and time has passed with us truly realizing it. We take time for granted like we will always have some, only to forget we only have so much and none of us know how much we have left, but we don't think about that. We can't see it so it keeps going by right in front of us. So many of us fill in our time like filling a ditch with dirt. We look for things to pass our time with. When we do this, we have no respect for time, it's just another way of wasting our time. If we were to become aware of how precious time is, then perhaps we could make better use of it. When a person is given say only three months to live, their time becomes very precious to them. They will spend more time with those they love. They will spend their time doing something meaningful and beneficial, not only to them but to people in general. This poem was written to make us aware that since we have so little time in the scheme of things, we

should try to at least make our time account for something
and to be spent in love.

## Only So Many Years

We only have so many years
So many years, so many tears
So little time so many mistakes
So little time so few good breaks

Our world, this world is over
Billions of years old
Why must we live some or most
Of our time with hearts so cold
We only have so much life
Why spend it tormented by strife?

None of us have a guarantee of tomorrow
But too many of us live our last day in sorrow
With regrets for the wrongs we have done
And the hurt we have caused our loved ones
Why do we keep on hurting with so many
Of our years already gone?

Seeking God, searching for something or someone
To which we can belong
Deep down we realize and know
That we must at some time reap what we sow

## Only So Many Years

Compared to the billions of years in time
Our life is like billions of dollars
Compared to less than a dime

Only so many years, so many seconds
Each one should count before our
Final fate beckons
Forget everything else, all we have is time

During our life, we always depend on how
We spend our little dime,
We only have so many years
Why the need for so many tears?

# Insight

The ability to see through and into people and situations is called insight. It all starts with one little word, "why". Why does a person behave that way? Why is this happening?

The person with insight is looking for the truth about people and occurrences. It's a process of considering many different options and examining each one until the "why" makes sense, even if it's not the answer you would like it to be. The person who strives for and achieves insight is not afraid of the truth, even when it becomes painful or destroys what they may have believed in with all of their heart.

The insightful person must have the capability to see the real, and have the mental discipline to accept what they see and the strength to bear it. The person with true insight is feared by those whose lives are a series of pretenses. They can fool and beguile many, but the person with insight will see through them. The hardest thing about being an insightful person, a truly insightful person, is that they can see through themselves as well. They seldom like what they see but know they have to change or live with it.

# Cheerful

Everyone likes to be around a cheerful person unless they are so unhappy with themselves that they can't stand to see someone else in a good mood. People feel better when in the company of a cheerful person because it makes them feel good, and in a lot of ways it's contagious.

Someone who is usually cheerful will try to stay that way even when there might not be anything to be cheerful about. It's their way of dealing with a bad situation or hard times. You would never even know anything was wrong in their life unless they confessed it to you.

Cheerful people must have a positive attitude to remain that way because there is always enough happening in life which could be considered anything but cheerful. They take the good and the bad in strides without losing a beat. Cheerful people have most likely been that way all of their lives. It's a habit, a good habit, but a habit none the less. Those of a cheerful disposition can make you feel better just by being around them. Whether the cheer is real or contrived cheerfulness, it has the power to lift people up.

# Silence

Silence can be a human being's greatest refuge. A place to retreat where they are not bombarded by physical stimulation. A place where they can retire to collect their thoughts with no artificial interference. Silence provides an environment for reflective thinking, where one's own thoughts can be put into an objective perspective. Silence is the best way to get in touch with your spiritual side.

Silence is rest time for your soul, a time out for your spirit without the distractions of the physical world. Silence is also very effective in a heated emotional situation, since it allows a person to think and then act rather than not thinking and only reacting. Silence is a tremendous educational tool. When you are talking, you cannot learn. It is only when you remain silent that you can concentrate on what is being taught and absorb it.

Last but not least, silence is the bridge between mind and spirit. Silence will enable a person to reach out and perhaps touch the essence of their being.

# Candid

What's the big difference between being candid and being frank? Frank is blunt and often thoughtless. A frank statement has no regards for the effect that it has on the listener. The brutal truth and nothing but the brutal truth is the essence of the frank statement. Feelings are not considered at all and sensitivity put aside.

A candid person, on the other hand, will tell you the truth of what they think but only if asked or prompted. The candid statement is somewhat couched in tactful language. The candid person is plain spoken but not brutally frank. The candid person is basically an honest person who will tell you how they really feel. Most people have a difficult time being candid since it is a lot harder to be honest with someone and tell them something they may not want to hear. Candid people are considered to be more sincere and genuine than a lot of people since they wish to help by telling the other person something that may help them resolve a problem or quandary.

## Candid

It's far better to seek the advice of a candid person rather than someone who is afraid to speak what they feel is the truth.

# Kim Wong and the Great Physics Mystery

A true story, only the names have been changed so that the people involved can retain their dignity.

It all began in a cemetery and ended in a cemetery, or did it?

A sales manager for a cemetery was talking to the owner one day. The owner suggested they go out into the cemetery and see if anyone was buried in a particular plot. The owner frequently forgot where he buried people. He took two coat hangers and bent them straight out and bent them again so he could grip them properly, and off he went into the cemetery holding tow coat hangers straight out. He came to the spot in question, and when he walked over it, the coat hangers crossed. He remarked that he had found the gravesite; as he walked on, the coat hangers went back straight out when he walked across an area where there were no burials.

# Kim Wong and the Great Physics Mystery

Years passed. The sales manager had moved on to bigger and better things. He formed a business deal with an associate named Kim Wong. He had never forgot about the coat hangers. Kim came from a wealthy family and had a doctorate degree, so when the sales manager told him the coat hanger story, Kim was in disbelief as most people would be. After stating his doubt several times, the sales manager suggested they get a pair of coat hangers and go to a local cemetery. When they got there, the sales manager bent the coat hanger straight. He walked along until he came to a grave and the coat hanger crossed and straightened out when he left the grave site.

"You made them cross," Kim said. The manager then suggested Kim try it himself. Kim walked along with the hangers straight out, and when he walked across the grave, the hangers crossed. He was in a state of disbelief, and when he walked along several more graves, the hangers crossed over each one. Kim asked his partner what was the principle behind this?

The sales manager said he had no idea. Kim insisted there must be a principle of physics that would explain all of this. Kim had gone to UCLA and knew a physics professor there. He said he would call the professor and find out the principle behind this. He phoned the professor and explained how he had taken two coat hangers, which were bent straight out and that they had automatically crossed when he walked over a grave. He asked the physics professor what principle was involved. There was a pause, a long silence, and then the professor said to him, "Kim, please seek professional help."

Kim was now in a complete state of quandary. He felt that he might go his whole life without the answer to what had now become a mystery to him.

# Cohesion

Some people "have it together." These are the ones that we speak of as having cohesion. They "have it all together" as a person. They are able to deal with almost any situation and retain their composure. They strike a balance between too much and too little. They blend into almost any social situation and can talk with others on almost any level.

They don't try too hard or try too little. They are usually moderate in most things and have a well-rounded social life, the most important being family. The person with a cohesive personality also sticks by their friends. People cling to them because they seem to be happy, well-adjusted and successful in what they do. Cohesive people are usually able to put themselves, others, and the world in perspective. They seem to know how everything looks and how it all fits together. When things seem at their worst, cohesive people seem at their best, for when all things are coming apart, they are keeping it all together.

# Simplicity

Some people, if not most, cry out to be recognized. They say by their words and actions, "Look at me, see how great I am" and "What a wonderful person I am." They put on airs, pretenses and showiness. They strive for recognition by being strong, wealthy, sexy, talented, smart, and creative. Their life is spent trying to impress others by any means they can. They brag and bully. They act mean, sad, happy, and humble. It's all an act to entertain and manipulate.

Their opposite is the person of simplicity who has no need to impress others or to achieve recognition. Their lives are noticeably different for their lack of affection or pretense. They have no need for showiness of any kind. Luxury and high connections hold little to no interest for them. Their tastes in everything are fairly simple. They enjoy simple food and simple pleasures. It doesn't take much to make them happy. They are content with very little. Their lives are built around the enjoyment of the natural in life. Simplistic people have discovered the true meaning of life and live in its depth.

# The Only Thing

One of the most important facts of life, if not the most important to know, is one very simple thing. The only thing and the one thing that you will ever have complete control over is what you think. Repeat. The only thing you have any control over is what you think. You cannot control other people, you can only manipulate and influence them. You can't control them.

You cannot control events that happen around you, the best you can hope for is to be able to spot trouble and stay out of the way. Therefore, the world we live in, we have no control. Once you realize that you can control things and how they affect you, you can control what you think and choose to not let it affect or impact you.

If you choose to think that someone has hurt you, and you choose to think that you will get even or you choose to let any other emotion control your thoughts, then you have not controlled your thoughts. You would have if you wanted to. You have chosen to let the event and your reaction control you. You can control what you think and better control the situation.

## Some Men Can Only Love Men

Some men can love only another man
And on this society has placed a ban
They may truly love and care in a special way
But no matter how beautiful the word is still gay

Laws and custom will not hinder love
Provided it is between the opposite gender
Sex is limited and has its bounds
So says those who own and run the towns

A combination of young and old
Receive a shoulder which is cold
The act of love between sister and brother
Is sure to get you in trouble one way or another

Making love is therefore only allowed
For prescribed pairs, all other is disavowed
But wish as they may and try and they might
When love becomes true
Nothing or no one can reach its height

# The Truth

The truth, the real truth, may be as elusive as a puff of cigarette smoke. Most people don't want to know the truth, anyway. It's too painful, too hard to accept and deal with about ourselves, others and situations. It's too easy to believe the lies we are told every day. The lies are comforting, creating the illusion that everything is all right and if it's all right, we can cope. We can't cope with a truth that is beyond our power to do anything about and has the potential to hurt us, kill us, deprave us or cause us great harm.

In fact, society as we know it could not function if the truth were told. Suppose manufacturers told us that they deliberately produce products that are designed only to last a short time so that we will have to buy more? What if we were told that the guarantees we get are legally worded to so that we 1. Would not understand them and 2. Contained legal loopholes that would allow the guarantor to get out of the warranty easy?

## The Truth

Suppose we were told that a war is only for the purpose of a few people to make a lot of money. Would we send our sons to die for an oil company or defense contractors? What if insurance companies would tell us that they will use every tactic possible to not pay or pay less or as little as they have to even though they should? Would we truly want to know and if we did, would we buy as much? How would we change our lives?

The is a saying, which we have all heard, and that is "the truth shall set you free." Not so fast. You can look in the mirror and tell yourself the truth about who and what you are if you have the moral strength to do that. You can admit, "I'm an alcoholic." Does this truth set you free from being an alcoholic? I'm afraid not. The only thing that will set you free from alcohol is a choice to develop a mindset never to drink again.

Truth is probably one of the most aligned concepts there is. Each religion has its own truth, so do political parties and any all organizations, as well as each individual. What is mistaken for the truth is actually a belief. The truth is a totally undeniable 100% fact, and there are very few of these around. We can search for the truth.

There are really only two truths. One is flawed with the inability to tell the truth about yourself, so it may not be absolute. The only absolute truth is that we start to die the minute we are born and that we will all die. Period.

# Knowledge is Power

An expert is said to be someone who knows one more fact than you about something. The advantage of knowing more, even a little more, is enough for a person to take control of the situation. Control is predicated upon, revealed, or it relies on someone with the audacity and/or confidence and no inhibition about taking control.

Another way knowledge is shown or used is when someone is able to demonstrate that they know more about the situation, or they know how to organize and solve the problem at hand. The more knowledge a person has in relation to other people, the more power they have. The example of a doctor and his patient illustrates that point. The doctor possesses far superior medical knowledge and therefore controls the relationship and treatment.

Someone who knows the solution to a grave problem when no one else does holds the ultimate power. The use of this power, however, must be safeguarded by the sole retention of the knowledge-haver. If the person gives away his knowledge, he gives away his power.

## Beware the Smile

Beware the smile and toothy grin
Your body and mind are the prize they hope to win
A glad hand and a pat on the back
Usually means you have something they lack

Beware of those who speak with someone else's voice
You may find you will be given a choice
Accept what they say and never doubt
Or you may question, but you will do without

Beware of those who speak with someone else's words
You may find yourself in one of many herds
The verbs, prepositions, adjectives, and nouns
Will be used to extract your flesh by the pound

# How Do You Know What is Right?

Whether you have a conscious or not, or whether you believe you have a conscious or not, a tiny little voice from down deep inside of you will tell you if something is wrong, and if it's not wrong, the chance is that it is right.

It's right when the thought of doing it brings you joy and happiness not merely pleasure and excitement, but true joy. Only that which is right can create that kind of joy from within, everything else will only give you momentarily pleasure. People do things that make them feel good, but they may not be right such as getting even with someone by doing something which will cause them pain and embarrassment. It is not right to do this, but it does make you feel; however, it will never bring you joy and true happiness because it was not right.

Innately, we can tell if something is right, the same way we can tell if something is wrong.

# Imagination is More Important Than Knowledge

Anyone can gain knowledge if they choose to apply themselves, but not everyone is born with imagination. Imagination is the key to the discovery of the new. Imagination is also used to improve or change things and even people.

Knowledge on the other hand is old, the product of past imagination. Imagination is the key to progress and advancement, whether it be in the arts or the sciences. Leaders in their field have been blessed with active imaginations. They can see things others can't see through their imaginative ideas and dreams.

If they relied solely upon knowledge, no new advances could be had. It all begins with the imagination, which produces the ideas, which are then put on paper and finally created with whatever materials they need.

**Imagination is More Important Than Knowledge**

The greatest battleship began with the imagination of just one man, in the way of an example. The ability to see something that has never been is greater than knowing what already is.

# There Can Be No Security Where There Is Fear

## –Felix Frankfurter

Those who possess true inner security, the kind that no one can take away and allows one to endure anything, can only be present if there is no fear in your heart. Fear acts like an inhibitor that not only prevents you from doing things, it prevents you from being who you were meant to be. Fear can and does paralyze the mind and soul.

It represents freedom or can compare to slavery of sorts. When you have true security within yourself, you have freedom. Not the kind of freedom where you can do anything you want no matter what, but freedom in the sense that you will not become the slave of circumstances. Most people look for security from other sources than themselves. They

## There Can Be No Security Where There Is Fear

believe that other people institutions, corporations, govern-
ments, money and or power will give them security. It is an
illusion and its temporary at best.

Way down deep they know something is missing and
they feel insecure. Security comes from within not from
without.

# Uncle Coz

You knew instantly Coz wasn't right. It really wasn't hard to see. He was disheveled and his hair was wild. His eyes darted constantly, and when he spoke, nothing made any sense. His nose was broken and twisted to one side. His jaw stuck out and there were flat spots where his cheek bones should have been.

"Hey, what's going on? I got to get to the place, need something. Gotta go now. What's the matter? Nothing the matter. Gotta go."

This was typical conversation for Coz. He lived with a widowed sister and brother in the Hill District. They lived on a small street house on Cliff Street, which got its name because in the back of the house on the street, there was a cliff which dropped a few hundred feet. From their back porch they had a panoramic view of downtown Pittsburgh. They had lived on the Hill since they were kids growing up. Ralph, Coz, and Emily. Emily and Ralph took care of Coz. He needed a lot of taking care of.

# Uncle Coz

Coz hadn't always been that way. When he was in his twenties, Coz was handsome, smart, and possessed a charisma which attracted women by the score. He was a dapper debonair dresser and the envy of most guys on the Hill. Coz always had money. He was one of the sharpest gamblers in the city. He won at cards and could figure the odds correctly on almost any sporting event for boxing and baseball. Coz had it all.

Then one day, he met a girl, a beautiful girl. He fell madly in love, and she fell madly in love with him. They would steal precious moments together. They had to. She was the girlfriend of the richest boss in the Hill. He was a boss of the syndicate operating in the Hill and downtown. He controlled all of the illegal gambling and prostitution in his jurisdiction. He was powerful, and he commanded an army of thugs, tough guys, enforcers and yes, killers. This is why Coz and the woman had to sneak around. They had to be careful. The boss was insanely jealous, vengeful, and of course, very violent.

They weren't careful enough. They were found out. They would always get together at a house that belonged to a friend of Coz. There were there together one night making love as they always did. Suddenly and without warning, the boss crashed through the door, accompanied by a half dozen or more of his tough guys, the two of them were defenseless. Screaming, shouting, and cursing ensued. Several of the tough guys held Coz. The boss pulled out a razor-sharp stiletto, and while two of his goons held the girl, he cut her face up one side and down the other. He then smashed her nose and mouth with his big ham first. She wasn't beautiful any more. This wasn't enough for him. He had his boys take turns raping her in every possible way while he forced Coz to look on.

Now it was Coz's turn. The enforcers took out their blackjacks and beat Coz's face and head to a pulp. They broke most the bones in his face and fractured his skull in several places. They took the girl away and forced her to be a prostitute in a whore house. They dragged Coz stark naked out in the street and thew him in the gutter. They say it was a miracle that he lived. Perhaps that was by design. But live he did, minus his looks and brains. They had literally beat his brains in.

He was mentally impaired for the rest of his life. There were times though that he would stare into space blankly and repeat over and over "Angie, Angie, Angie". Angie was his love. They say she died of a drug overdose. Nobody knows for sure. Coz spent the rest of his life being taken care of by his brother and sister, but he never forgot Angie.

# He Is Only Bright That Shines By Himself

## –George Herbert

Some bask in the glow of other people. They let their light shine on them. They are but moons reflecting the light of the sun. They have no light of their own. Someone who creates their own light has no need for the light that emanates from others. These individuals, however, are few and far between. Their accomplishments and their personality create a glow all of its own. They are truly shining examples of not only what is, but also of what could be.

Others can create their own light if only they would be themselves and enjoy their own endeavors, whatever they may be. We are all too much in the habit of trying to imitate others and create what they have so we too can shine, not

## He Is Only Bright That Shines By Himself

realizing that if we imitate others, our light will always be secondary and dimmer whereas our own original light, whatever that may be, will always be brighter.

## Love is Love and Nothing Else

Love is love and nothing else
When the other is number one
Or you consider the other before yourself,
And what ever they ask will be done

Be that woman and woman
Or be they man and man
Or be they any combination of one, two or more
Love is love if for each other they stand

Sharing becomes a thrill and joy
It doesn't have to be a girl and boy
It can be a pure love for yourself
If true concern and empathy is felt

Negatives are banished, the positives reign
Many words are spoken, but never to complain
Smiles abound and your joy is let out
Fear is unknown, for there is no doubt

Love yourself first, I strongly advise
You have to like yourself before

### Love is Love and Nothing Else

Another's love you can comprise
Loving yourself is no crime or cover
For unless you like you, you can like no other

# Enjoy Your Own Life Without Comparing it to that of Another

If you must compare your life with another, then it would be best to choose someone who has less. Most people compare their life to someone who has more and then they are envious, frustrated, or disappointed. This of course is a form of self-destructive behavior. The saying to "enjoy your life to the fullest" means to concentrate on the life you have, its joys, pleasures, and blessings – and they are many if a person would only stop and look at what they have and be grateful.

For whatever reasons, you were not meant to have the kind of life that you may compare your own life with. Your life can be exciting, fulfilling, and joyous if you can accept it in its totality. The most important thing to remember is that you have a life which is God's greatest gift to you. You exist and are part of something great, wonderful, and eternally divine, and you were meant to do and be something special. It's up to you to find out what that is and do it.

If you do that, you will not have the time or inclination to compare yourself to anyone.

# Is it possible to Live Authentically?

Authentic means real, so the question is can a life be real and genuine? For a life to qualify for this, then what a person says must be real. He must speak what he thinks. This is possible but it is impractical since the peace of life comes from diplomacy. He must also act realistic and this presents a problem since most actions are based on emotion and do not conform to the reality of the situation.

A person is told that he can't have or do something. The reality of that situation is a simple fact, but most people cannot accept this authentic fact and become frustrated and react. This is not real or authentic behavior according to the situation. Authentic behavior would be to expose the thoughts, feelings, or the person and have them inhibit their true feeling in place of reacting accordingly to their human nature. When something is authentic, it is beyond reproach and this is impossible for a human to achieve even on a temporary basic much less their whole life.

# A Good Leader is a Good Follower

There's an old army saying that goes, "you have to be able to take orders before you can give orders." In other words, you must experience being under someone. This does two things – it shows that you are able to accept discipline and so that when you are told something, you understand when you must put yourself aside and do what is good for the organization. It also is so that you know how it feels to be under someone, so that when you have someone under you, you will know how it feels and your judgment and awareness will be keener.

A good leader must have empathy for those who follow him. He must be humble in the fact that he was at one time a follower, also some men step into the position of leadership without ever having the benefit of being beneath another person. They usually make the worse leader since they have little or no understanding of what it feels like to be a follower.

## Push Comes to Shove

Push always seems to come to shove
The young use snotty words and preach love
Understanding is supposedly the word of the day
But the young still refuse to let any other have a say

Prejudice is a no-no if you are under twenty-eight
The young are not biased, the old just fail to relate
Give to me and do for me, but I don't owe you a thing
The young call the giver and the doer a ding-a-ling

The world owes us oh so much
The young tell everyone who's good for a touch
Sex is supposed to be bonded with love and real
    meaning
But young men are forever discussing seduction,
    scheming

The search for truth is constantly taking place
The young like everyone else, lie to save their face
Money is said to have no importance of its own
So why do the young keep what they have,
And when it's gone they moan and groan

# How Do Evil and Suffering Fit into the Divine Plan?

Evil is a byproduct of good. If there was no good, there could be no evil. One spawns the other. When a good is done, an evil is produced to counter it, and when an evil is done, a good is produced to counter it.

Suffering is a byproduct of evil, which is necessary for good to exist. This is the divine plan for good to eventually prevail, which it does; however, it produces evil in the pattern. This balance and counter balance exists due to the nature of the material world, which could not exist without conflicting and opposing forces. When something arises, be it good or evil, an opposing force will be produced to counter it. It is nature and the natural law of the material word in which we happen to live.

**How Do Evil and Suffering Fit into the Divine Plan?**

Suffering is inevitable. It cannot be avoided. It is a result of the process, but put into the proper context, it can be a blessing or good if it makes a person wiser or gives them insight and teaches a lesson that could not be learned otherwise. When this happens, then things even like suffering have happened for the best. Good prevails.

# The Clergy

Perhaps this is too harsh and critical of the clergy, but it is true to some degree of all clergy. They share a life where security is promised, and conflict is at a bare minimum. They truly do lead a peaceful life with lots of perks. Some deserve it, and some don't. people tend to put their trust in the clergy, which allows them the ability to take advantage of the circumstances or to actually perform criminal acts such as the sexual abuse of children, which has taken place all too often. The worse crime, however, is that the church hierarchy covers this up and allows it to continue so that the church will not be subject to low sects and criminal prosecution along with the loss of trust. What is lost in all of the adoration of priests and all clergy is that we are all God's children and all share the same moral dilemmas. When we place others above us, we automatically place ourselves below them. Thus, we are all of God's children – If people could only see that, no one is above or below anyone, we are just different. If we could look at others that way, we would understand God did not make us to judge or be judged. If we could only accept ourselves and others as God's children and nothing more.

## The Clergy

Oh, to be one of the special people
Let's make everyone in the world a clergy
And release us all from physical drudgery
Make everyone in the world secure
So each and every one can act demure

Give us our daily bread
And keep a roof above our head
Then give us a parish car
So we can travel near and far

Release our minds from fear of need
Filter our brains so we don't want to breed
Keep our bellies full and our bodies warm
And put us in a safe place free from harm

Give us time to think and meditate
Let us think our thoughts and contemplate
Our being is free and we can smile
At everyone as we walk up our church aisle

## The Clergy

We can refresh ourselves and then relax
Because after all we don't pay tax
Thus we have such money to blow,
To build ornate churches to house our own ego

We would dispense our good advice
Then reassure our flock their donations suffice
We would greet all with a pleasant look
Then go right back to reading our book

Some would say we were too smug and complacent
Others would say that to God we were adjacent
We would listen to the trouble of a mother
And prescribe clichés of one sort or another

A smile would be branded on her face
After all we would be in a state of heavenly grace
Gone to God's good work, we would say
And when you're in trouble all we can do is pray

Get a nickel and a dime from each of the poor
Get a piece of the action from those with a little more
Keep the church building but buy a new door
Save a couple dollars and find a discreet whore

Preach that God will come sometime
But until he does, I'll make sure I get mine

## The Clergy

Heaven and Hell and the Holy Ghost
Can be used to batter our sheep from pillar to post

Guilt and shame, we can constantly dispense
Remembering to keep the masses on the defense
But oh my god, I just happen to recall
We are God's children one and all

# Can We Pursue a Common Good?

We can and we should pursue a common good in the interest of progress. Unless a society continues to make progress, it will degenerate and fail. Progress is only possible when something like the common good has been achieved. A common good is necessary for harmony and harmony is the way to progress.

If one segment of society is in conflict with another segment of society to the point that one is infringing on the basic rights of the others, then progress is impossible. When some in society are stepping on the tails of others, then progress can never be achieved. The common good unites all where they march together in progress, united, as opposed to becoming lost in conflict and the symbolic stepping on tails.

The common good is exactly what it says and means. It is the good that results from everyone having basic rights and feeling secure in their value.

# History Repeats Itself

If you want to predict what will happen and a similar circumstance in history, no matter how long ago, occurred with similar circumstances, then you will end up with an idea of what the result will be. A prime example is a civil conflict in a country between two factions. When another country enters the conflict and takes sides in order to establish a presence, the result will be a defeat for the foreign entity. This happened with the French in Vietnam. Had the United States studied the history of that defeat, they would have realized that no matter how powerful they were, they could not win a guerrilla war in a foreign country. It was a disaster for the U.S.

And then thirty years later, still not having learned the lessons of history, they became involved in another civil guerrilla war in Iraq, again with disastrous consequences. They fell into the same trap in Afghanistan.

The only question that remains is are the leaders stupid, or do they just want a war?

# Mind over matter

Dewey would say to Brian on many occasions, "Life is mind over matter, if you don't mind, it doesn't matter." Brian always thought this was funny and would laugh. Dewey would just smile and say, "Someday you'll understand."

Brian moved to another city. Dewey kept on helping as many people as he could. He would frequently say, "So much to do, so little time to do it." He felt like he had much more to do, but he knew his time was growing short. He studio was above a popular delicatessen in downtown. It was open late. Dewey would go down after his last appointment and have a cup of coffee. One night, he went down for his regular cup of coffee. The waitress came back to the table to see if he wanted a refill. Dewey had laid his head on his arms as if he were asleep. The waitress left and came back after a while. It was getting close to closing time, so she tried to wake Dewey up. Dewey was not to be woken up this time. He had died.

Dewey was a prolific writer and left box full after box full of private writings in his studies. He never shared these with anyone. His wife Mattie had the job of clearing out his belongings. She packed all of his writing up and took them to a lawyer to look over. This was the life work of a very unique man who had insights into human nature and the nature of material things that very few people had, if any. The lawyer started to read Dewey's writing and after a while, turned to Mattie and said, "This is the work of the devil and must be destroyed."

Mattie was a simple person and the lawyer was an educated professional. He must have known better. She agreed and both of them fed this brilliant man's life work into the fire. God only knows what secrets he had discovered and unlocked. All gone. Brian found out about his death a year or so after he died. Several years later, he had to go back to the city. Mattie had died in the meantime. Brian knew where they were buried because Dewey had told him his arrangements for burial before he left town.

Brian went to the cemetery office, found out the grave's location and went to pay his final respects to his dearest friend and second father. There they lay together in death as in life. Brian read the words on Dewey's tombstone.

"Life is mind over matter, if you don't mind, it doesn't matter."

Brian smiled. It had taken him over twenty years to figure out what it meant. Dewey would have been pleased that it had finally dawned on Brian. After all, it was his favorite saying and the core of his life.

# Prelude – Never Ending

There are times in our lives when a confluence of emotions and events take place and create a dynamic which only grows strange through time and realization until it haunts you without surrendering. It will not let go and you can't let it go. It reaches the point when you even stop trying and accept it as your fate. It then becomes your daily ritual to ask God for forgiveness throughout the day, knowing he forgives but the dynamic goes on.

## Never Ending

Sometimes we want to talk to the dead
To tell them things that were never said
When they were here
To tell them how dear
They were to us and how much we regret

### Prelude – Never Ending

Not fulfilling expectations they had for us,
And which we never met–
They went to their grave thinking
We had ruined our life

They had many hardships and much strife
But there could have been no greater sorrow
Than to die with the thought that her son had no
　　tomorrow
There is no way that we can ever take back
Yesterday, so we live day-to-day
With the fact, that our mother's heart we did break

Though these worries we cannot shake,
We know and believe God forgives our sins
But we still must live with our heart
And mind and truth of what lies within

## The Only Reason

Life always leads to death
We are closer to the grave with each breath
We only seem to be alive
When we struggle to survive
We are all put here for a reason
And each part of our life is but a season

And each brings a new chance
To get past ourselves and enhance
Our lives and to bring out the good
In all of us which should
Bring us to fully realize and grasp
The true meaning and to know at last

What God has called us to do and be
So that we might be able to see
That each life plays a part in God's plan
And what happens to us is in God's hands

## The Dance of Death

Come dance with me, death would say
You may beg off for now,
But you will have to someday
I'll hold you in my arms
While you start to expire
I'll even let you have one heart's desire
Maybe and maybe not
That's up to me
You knew this moment would come
And now here I am
Would you like to tango,
Go out with a dramatic flair
Or would you like to waltz
And go out as gracefully as you can
Or would you like to do the two step
And just let me come and take you
Or would you like to dance fast,
And gyrate with all of your limbs twitching
Or would you like to dance slow,
I'll slow dance with you
It will be something akin to a romantic moment
I'll hold you close and caress you
Dance with me
And I'll take you into another world

# King of Hearts

We all have three hearts. We have the physical heart in our body. We also have a heart that is able to produce an intangible called love. Lastly, we have another heart that is also intangible, but it keeps us going without giving up no matter what the odds are or what and how strong the opposition. This is simply called heart.

Our physical heart provides an uninterrupted supply of food, oxygen and other essentials to every cell in our body. The heart is so powerful that it can pump the body's entire blood volume of 10 pints through the entire body about once a minute. It beats 70 times a minute and can increase this when the body is more active. Over a lifetime of 70 years, the heart beats some 2.5 billion times without tiring or stopping for a rest. This is truly the miracle muscle in our body.

## King of Hearts

Now comes the question. Which one of these three is
    the king of hearts?
The physical heart which keeps on beating until you
    take your last breath.
The heart of love which gives their body and soul to
    another or others.
Or the heart of hearts which goes beyond courage into a
    realm of the impossible.
There can only be one king.
That king is the physical heart since it gives and sustains
    life, without which the two other hearts could not
    exist.

## King of Hearts

The literal kind of heart could be called heart of the heart. When someone says, "That person has real heart," it is the highest of compliments. It describes someone who is like our physical heart that keeps on going no matter what. It's the person who has been beaten but keeps on fighting or the person who is on a team with a scare that can never be overcome in the last remaining minutes but plays as hard as they did at the start of the game. It's the person who despites all of the odds against them, will give it his all until nothing is left. It's the person who may be physically beaten but never mentally beaten. It's the courage to keep going when there is no hope. If you have true heart, you will never be afraid of anything.

## King of Hearts

One time it was thought that the heart was the source of love and emotion. People used to and still do put their hand over their heart to express a feeling of love. The physical heart however produces no love or emotion. The feeling of love comes from deep inside of us. A mother's love for instance cannot be explained. It can be felt like no other love.

You can love someone and never understand why or you can love some for the traits they have such as someone who is kind, generous, humble, and loving. You can be loved and never truly appreciate how much you are loved. The greatest love there is will be unconditional love. When a person can love another person no matter what they say or do and no matter who they are or pretend to be and sustain that love no matter how badly they are treated or abused and still have love in their heart for that person that's unconditional love. It's rare, and the vast majority of people can only aspire to have that kind of love.

Love doesn't come from the heart, it comes from the soul.

# Self Assessment

## Who Are We

No matter who we are, we all have behavior problems of one kind or another. It helps us to know ourselves better if we are able to identify our behavior problems.

## Self Assessment

You now need to know what has happened in your life
that has caused you to have these problems.

You need to go into yourself to find out.
The answer lies within you.

Who has been the most important person in your life?
Who has influenced you the most?
What event stands out the most in your life?
What has been the worst thing that has happened to
you?
What is the best thing that has happened to you?
Who was the person in your life that made you feel the
best about yourself?

The things that have happened to you both good and
bad
and the people in your life both good and bad have
made
you who you are today. Each of your problems have a
solution and you have a choice, stay the way you are or
change what you want to. You must believe in
something
outside of yourself and you must believe in yourself. A
better life can be yours for the taking.

## Earthly Eternal Flame

He had to let go
Everyone has to go
It's just a question of time
It was his time
There was his body on the grill
God only knows where his spirit waited
The molecules had started to decay
Not many were going to stay
The flames were turned on
The process had begun
His body started to curl
Like a piece of paper on fire
He appeared to sit up
That's when it started to begin
The air forced from his lungs
Fire driven through his vocal cords
And a piercing shrill yell
Came out like a voice straight from hell
His body gone up and dropped like cigarette smoke
He had become a pile of ashes and bone
Which were ground up
And added to the pile he had become

## Earthly Eternal Flame

Earthly fire was turned into an eternal flame
He was now on an eternal plane
Only his ashes and his memory were to remain

## Fire in Her Eyes

She was a plain person
She looked plain
She dressed plain
And she wore glasses
Which hid her eyes
But every once in a while
She would come out
The plain disappeared
And off came the glasses
Mascara and eyeshadow appeared
Rouge and bright red lipstick
Changed her into someone no one knew
A man would catch her eye
She would stare so intensely
That something in him made him turn and look
The pent-up passion in her eyes was like fire
He couldn't move
She melted him like wax on a hot stove
I'm yours, take me, now
Her eyes could talk and seduce
This helpless man in front of her
He fell into her web and got lost
In the clutches of this plain woman

# The Messenger

He came to the door
He was just the messenger
The door opened
He said he had some bad news
"Your husband is dead"
It was the most direct way it could be said
The wife stared straight ahead
Oh my God, he's dead
She didn't even know where to start
The messenger stood silent at the door
It was obvious he could do no more
She closed the door and sat down
Her emotions were spinning around
An emotional tide of sorrow swept over her
She broke down unable to control the tears
They were together at the start of the day
And now on a cold steel gurney he lay
He lay on this cold steel gurney unable to say

## The Messenger

That she was his one true love
He could say it but no one could hear it
But she couldn't hear him say
Because on a cold steel gurney he lay
He was gone either up or down below
She would not be able to let him know
How much she loved him and be able to show
Her love with one last kiss
And now left with only deep regret that she did miss
Her last chance to show him her love
Before he was taken from her to the above

# Just a Theory and Some Conjecture on Sadism and Masochism

One coin: two sides – Sadism and Masochism

## Sadism

The majority of people in prison, probably over 70%, have been molested or abused as children. Obviously, this has had a dramatic impact on their lives. As a result, they have gone into themselves. They care only what happens to them. They have lost a connection to other people and have become selfish. They have lost the ability to care for other people. They are unaffected by what happens to others. They are in the grip of a subconscious fear and use aggression and overcompensation to alleviate this fear. There is also a subconscious feeling of rejection, causing a "beat first" mechanism combined with a get-even mindset. This leads to unwarranted hostility and violence. The feeling of projecting their pain upon others makes them feel superior and it makes them feel good to see others in pain.

They have gotten to the point where even other people's pain seems to erase their own sense of inferiority, and since they are not capable of having an emotional connection to others, they don't care what happens to other people. It doesn't bother them to see others in pain, in fact, they enjoy it. Again, it makes them feel good. They can hurt people in a number of ways both physical and mental by what they say and do, and some even become child molesters and keep the chain of sadism going.

It is a well-known fact that when someone goes to prison for pedophilia, that they have to be put in a separate unit or confinement for their own protection. There was an instance where a priest was put in prison for pedophilia, and someone who had been brutally molested as a child somehow managed to get assigned to the same cell as the priest. He found a way to fix the door where no one could come in. He then tied up the priest, got on the top bunk, and jumped down on the priest's stomach from the top bunk repeatedly. No one could get into the cell to save the priest. This was an ultimate example of both sadism and revenge. Sadism has at its base a sense of complete and total inferiority.

## Masochism: The Other Side of the Coin

The last line on the basis of sadism was that sadists have a sense of complete and total inferiority. Inflicting pain on others makes them feel good. The masochist enjoys having pain inflicted on them, physical in some who are classic masochists, but for the most part, mental. They too have been abused for the most part mentally, but for some physically and mentally. They have no sense of no self-worth. They feel a need to be punished for having no worth. When they were children, they were told they were worth nothing and that they'd never amount to anything. They may have been called stupid and unable to learn anything, or they may have been berated and called nothing but a little slut. Girls were more vulnerable to this than boys.

Boys were abused both ways and grew a rage to get even. They became sadists. Girls often went the other way. When other people put them down, it was like receiving a form of attention and it made them feel good. They were noticed. Someone cared enough about them to belittle or berate them; after all, they had no sense of self-worth. They would choose abusive husbands who abused them sexually and verbally. They would choose as friends people who were always making fun of them. They enjoyed playing the inferior role. After all, they were made to feel inferior and fit right into the part in their minds. Their life was hell because they could not control their situations. They didn't even want to. They made the best sexual slaves and those who ran the sexual slave rings would look for the signs and characteristics of the typical masochist. They met all of the criteria. Mental anguish and pain of almost any sort were welcome. They had fulfilled their destiny, which was to feel worthless.

## The Middle Ground

There are degrees in everything, including sadism and masochism. There are some people who are just a little sadistic and some who are just a little masochistic. A sense of inferiority still fuels those who whose are just a little sadistic and who are just a little masochistic.

## The Best of Both Worlds

There are some people who are a combination of both sadistic and masochistic. One example would be gamblers. They are a perfect combination. When they lose, they feel they are being punished and have had something taken away from them. When they win, they feel like they have "gotten one over on someone" and have caused them pain because they have taken something from them. The beautiful part of being a gambler is that they can't lose. If they win, they win. If they lose, they win, so no matter how it goes, they come out winners. For the most part, this fills subconscious desires. People who are truly sadistic and masochistic feel this on a conscious level. The real truth is everyone on a subconscious level is a tiny bit sadistic or a tiny bit masochistic, or sometimes both.

# Total Humiliation

Sometimes Dewey would hypnotize people he liked just to get rid of a minor problem. Someone might casually mention that they had an ache or pain or some other minor ailment. That was all it took for Dewey to swing into action. He would say, "I'll take care of that for you" and proceed to deploy a hypnotic method.

Every Saturday, after swimming class was over, Brian would ride into town on the streetcar with Dewey. The streetcar was open about halfway with a long seat on each side. In the back were seats with two on each side facing front. Dewey always sat on the long seat. One Saturday afternoon as they were riding into town, Brian casually mentioned that me had warts on two of fingers.

"Warts," Dewey explained, "that's easy to take care of. Here, give me your hand."

Dewey took Brian's hand and in a strong distinct voice said, "Wart, wart, go away."

## Total Humiliation

The attention of everyone on the street including the conductor was riveted on them. Dewey continued, in a voice heard by all, "Wart, wart go away." He continued to repeat the phrase.

Brian was looking for a hole to climb into or something to hide behind, but he couldn't stop Dewey.

"Wart, wart go away."

Brian was hoping that himself and the wart would disappear. It didn't happen, but two days later the warts were gone. Even the wart would not withstand the humiliation and disappeared. Dewey had no idea that he had embarrassed Brian so bad that he would never forget it.

# Flat Line

That fateful day had finally come
The life he had, now there was none
He knew that someday he would hear
That he had no life, but never thought it near
The flat line said there was no more
It was good because life had become a bore
Those who loved him all had fears
And losing him reduced them to tears
Now he was never again going to be around
The flat line was to take away the sound
Of his voice and all the things he could say
Since the flat line made it his last day
His future was gone and he could not begin
Again to promise God he would not sin
Anymore and do things that would
Cause someone pain and do the things he should
Have done all of his life
The flat line had just ended his strife

# Beyond Death

"Don't anyone say he's dead," cautioned Dewey. He was about to do something he had done several times, if not many times, before. Dewey was going to put himself in a trance and cease all bodily functions. He would not only cease all breathing, his heart rate would be so low as not to even have a pulse. On this occasion, as something in the past, a doctor was on hand, usually out of curiosity. It was hard for medical men to believe that the human body could be shut down to that extent and not be dead, so they came to see for themselves. They saw, and what they saw absolutely amazed them.

Dewey would put himself in a trance and shut his body not only down, but off. When he would do this, the doctors would feel for a pulse, only not to find one. They would take out the stethoscope and listen for a heartbeat. If there was one it was not discernable. They would hold a cold piece of glass under his nose to catch the slightest hint of breath. None came. The glass did not condensate even ever so slightly. This is why Dewey would caution everyone not to say, "he'd dead."

Although it did appear for all intents and purposes that he was dead, since he was in a state of deep hypnosis, he was vulnerable to the slightest suggestion. His life was connected only by the thinnest of threads. If someone had said, "Oh my God, he's dead," he would have been. The suggestion would have been given, accepted, and obeyed, and he would have departed this world. The doctors could do nothing but shake their heads. They did not understand. Dewey programmed himself to come out of this death-like trance after a few minutes. He performed this feat to demonstrate the power of hypnosis. It worked. People came away with a newfound respect for the power of the subconscious mind.

Brian had seen him do this many times. One day, he asked Dewey not about where he went when he was in this death-like trance because he did not want to intrude on something he felt was very personal to Dewey, but he did ask, "What about death, Dewey?"

Dewey, without hesitation said, "There is nothing to fear."

Wherever he was during those times in the deep trance, he was literally disconnected from life. It was an experience which left him with an insight that gave him a peace rarely found in human beings. When he said to Brian "there is nothing to fear", he had a look in his eyes that transcended all worldly and natural things. It was a look of someone who had attained a complete peace within himself. Brian wished many times that he had asked him what he experienced in that trance; perhaps Dewey would have been able

## Beyond Death

to describe it or perhaps not. Brian, like most but not all people, feared death and the great unknown. When Dewey said there was nothing to fear with that look on his face and in his eyes, Brian never feared death after that.

# Where does love end and fucking begin

Where does love end and fucking begin?
What part of intercourse is labeled a sin
Who do we become when our pleasures control us
When do we turn from human being into pure animal
   lust?

The cock gets hard and spawns desire
The clitoris awakens and ignites a fire
The nipples become suddenly hard and firm
The quest is beginning to cause the body to yearn

A touch on the leg, a kiss on the lips
Each body responds to the caress of fingertips
The juices now cannot stop their flow
The heart is full, and the spirit is aglow

The lovers proceed to quench the awful thirst
And slowly begin to consider themselves first
Romance and fantasy fill the woman's head
Her feminine nature wants to submit to the man in her
   bed

## Where does love end and fucking begin

The sense of touch is used to its very best
Leg touches leg and breast lies against chest
Hands and lips; tongue and mouth know no boundaries
And their passion is released through animal sounds

A short quick thrust puts his cock inside
Her walls quiver as they feel his organ glide
Her eyes are closed but she sees herself just the same
She's now living a fantasy whose fulfillment is the aim

His strokes become harder and faster
His penis is now becoming his master
The semen that fills him is starting to surge
The animal we all have inside will now emerge

The woman reaches her orgasm again and again
The depths of her feelings, she'll never be able to
    comprehend
The waves of ecstasy that flow through her insides
Cause a tide she is unable to control or hide

Where does love end and fucking start
Fucking begins when feelings for the other person
    depart
Who do we become when pleasure controls us?
We become what in reality we are, animals of lust

# Dewey Deavers

Dewey Devers was born in 1897 in Paducah, Kentucky. He ran away and joined a traveling carnival when he was 14. The carnivals of those days had many different acts, among which were hypnotists, a martial arts expert, a strong man act, and a Geek. We'll come back to the geek a little later on. The hypnotist, martial arts expert, and strong man all took a liking to Dewey and taught him everything they knew. He married a woman named Mattie and moved to Pittsburgh and opened up a studio divided into two parts.

One half was for teaching hypnotism and doing hypnotherapy for people who had problems of shyness, sleeping, depression and other mental disabilities. Psychiatrists would also refer people to him who they felt helpless to cure, such as paranoids, sadists, masochists, and people with dual and multiple personalities. The other half of the studio had a mat that covered the entire floor. It was here that he taught boxing, wrestling, Judo, Jiu-Jitsu, kung fu, La Savate, which is French foot fighting, southern plantation head fighting and even dirty street fighting.

He never owned a car, and at 4 or 5 in the afternoon, he went by street car to the Boys Club of Pittsburgh where he taught swimming and life guard training. He worked 23 hours a day and hypnotized himself to where he would get eight hours of sleep in one hour. Usually, he worked six days a week and sometimes seven days. Dewey always wore a double-breasted suit and parted his hair in the middle. He would put on hypnotic acts where he would hypnotize people and hang them. A strong man art he performed before he came to Pittsburgh consisted of moving a boat load of 23 people across the widest part of the Ohio River, while being tied and fit with a harness as well as having large slabs of rock being broken by a sledge hammer while they were on top of his head.

Dewey and my father were good friends since they both come from Paducah, KY. My father died when I was ten and even though Dewey wasn't married to my mother, he became my father, my mentor and my best friend. He taught me all he knew. He was strong, kind, generous and had a sense of humor. He was truly a very unique person.

Oh, by the way, the Geek –
The Geek of the carnival was a guy usually kept in a cage. His act was to kill a live chicken and then eat it. Raw.

# Just a Thought

I believe in alien life. We live in a universe where there are millions of stars, which are just like our sun and also have planets revolving around them. The law of odds and probability are that hundreds, if not more, have the same ability to sustain life as we know it on Earth. We have made more progress in the last 100 years than the 6000+ before. We are on the cusp of going further than we ever dreamt of with computers and now A.I.

Imagine a planet similar to ours which possessed the same technology we have now, but which is a thousand years older. Imagine the technical position we have currently and the advances that could be made. The U.F.O are supposed to have technology which is beyond any on Earth. Suppose they do exist and are constantly observing us. More sightings have been seen since we exploded the first atomic weapon. China has vowed to be the greatest power in the world by 2049. Should they achieve this based on the fact they have a government which exerts total control over their own people and everything they are involved with, then it would be safe to assume they would look to control the entire world.

There is, however, the law of conflict, which assumes when a force that wishes to dominate, another force will come forth to oppose it. On a national scale, we call this war. There has already been two world wars. Why not a third? Each war becomes more destructive than the last. This being the case, the third will be more likely to be atomic with hydrogen bombs, which would make Hiroshima look like an artillery shell. Russia has over 5,000 atomic weapons on land, sea, and air. The U.S. has over 2,000. China has over 400. Great Britain, India, and a few other countries have them, as well. God only knows how many Israel has. This is well-kept secret. An atomic war would probably kill 99% of the people on the planet, as well as practically all animals and plant life due to radiation. It is said the cockroaches will be the last surviving life since they have the ability to adapt in one generation. This brings us back to the aliens, which may be watching us and what we are doing. By now, with their superior intelligence, they are aware that the human race is not advanced past the Neanderthal mind.

Should you come behind a professor of philosophy and put him in a deadly chokehold, his angry and violent nature will take over. The Neanderthal will take over. We are a planet of Neanderthals who are more than capable of destroying each other. The aliens must be aware of this. Now suppose that thousands or even hundreds of atomic weapons are detonated at the same time, we will not only destroy ourselves, we will release a storm of radiation upon the universe around us, which could have far-reaching effects on the other planets. The aliens with their superior intelligence and advancements would not allow this to happen. They would invade planet Earth and nullify our ability to destroy ourselves and other parts of the universe as well. Just a thought.

P.s. I believe that the aliens know who we are what we are, what we're doing, and possibly what we are thinking.

# Time

What is time? You can't see it. You can't touch or feel it, but it exists. We have it to spend. It belongs to us and what we do with it will determine our life. Once it's gone, it's gone. It's past time. We are presently living in present time, but it's fleeting and will soon be past time. We can look back on how we spent our time and learn from it.

We spend most of our time thinking. We average 2,000 to 3,000 thoughts per hour and we are what we think. Thoughts are things and they do materialize. Life is mind over matter, if you don't mind it won't matter. Simply put, our thoughts become our reality and that's where time comes in. We must have time to think and to think about what we do think. We only have so much time to do this because when we die, our time is up. This makes time our most precious commodity. Did you ever think about that when you waste your time as well all have done and will do? Those who waste most of their time wind up with wasted lives. It's our choice what we think and how we spend our time.

# Time

These two things will define our life for better or worse. We live in a world where time predominates. When we die our time is up. Should you believe in a spiritual life after death where there is no time, this is hard if not impossible to conceive.

## By the Balls

The medical establishment has you by the balls
They have total control and make all the calls
You have to do what they say when they say it
The best you can hope for is not to get a young twit
They have no regard for your time
The way they keep you waiting is a crime
They slice and they dice
And whatever the results, they don't even think twice
Forget the oath they had to take
It's all about the money they can make
Don't even think about getting their cell number
They are not about letting their patients encumber
Them and take up their time and pleasure
They do not feel responsible and this they treasure
We are at their mercy and their whim
They believe that their patients can either sink or swim
We all get sick at some time in our body
And the treatment we get is likely to be shoddy
Over doctors some people fawn
On some it may never even dawn
The medical establishment is just about the money
But when you wind up dead or crippled it's not funny

## By the Balls

Most people in the medical profession have a tendency
To treat you with no regard since you have a
    dependency
On them and they take full advantage of this
They have you by the balls in case you missed

## A Special Hell for the Old, Crippled, Confined, and Infirmed

It looks just like another building
From the outside you would never know what it's
    shielding
The light is blinking, it won't stop
A noise down the hall from that old grandpop
Let him wait, says one of the nurses
This is followed by a string of curses
He's probably in pain or something like that
So she just kept talking where she sat
The people she was to take care of didn't matter
She just kept on eating and getting fatter and fatter
The employees, most but not all, just didn't care
Of loving, kindness, and help they didn't share
Those who were confined were left to suffer
And after the friends and relatives left, there was no
    buffer
Then the staff could ignore them if they had a need
And the old, crippled, and infirmed could only concede
To whatever the staff wanted to do at the time
Which was to ignore the old, crippled, and confined
And leave their caretaking duties behind

## A Special Hell for the Old, Crippled, Confined, and In-

The old, crippled, and confined were wise not to make a
    sound
Or the staff could not be found
It was senseless to press the help light
Since forever they'd wait for staff to come into sight
Their food would arrive on a tray all mashed up
And unless they wanted to starve, this was their supper
Should they soil themselves all over, they'd sit for hours
    on end
Because no help would the staff send
This is the fate of the old, crippled, and confined
This is how the rest of their life would be defined

# Screams of the Dead

He lay on the grill all rigid and cold
He was without life, he had sold his soul
We had no idea who this was to be
We will have to die ourselves to see
The gas flames were turned on
In a few minutes his earthly body would be gone
He would then return to where he came
Without him the world would not be the same
The flames were now doing their job
His loved ones in another room began to sob
The flames were turning his body to dust
His bones were becoming but empty crusts
Like a dry leaf thrown in a fire, his body began to curl
He sat up as the fires started to unfurl
The air in his lungs was about to be forced out
Rendering a sound to curdle your blood, it was his last
    shout
It was over all too soon, leaving nothing but bones

## Screams of the Dead

Which were ground up in a machine that seemed to
  groan
His remains were now put in a ceramic vase
It would become harder and harder to remember his
  face
His ashes would be scattered to a bend
In a river where he was born, he was now but dust in
  the wind